Lyndon Baines *Johnson*

LYNDON BAINES *Johnson*

OUR THIRTY-SIXTH PRESIDENT

By Melissa Maupin

SPIRIT
of America™

The Child's World®, Inc.
Chanhassen, Minnesota

LYNDON BAINES *Johnson*

Published in the United States of America by The Child's World®, Inc.
PO Box 326 • Chanhassen, MN 55317-0326 • 800-599-READ • www.childsworld.com

Acknowledgments
    The Creative Spark: Mary Francis-DeMarois, Project Director; Elizabeth Sirimarco Budd, Series Editor; Robert Court, Design and Art Direction; Janine Graham, Page Layout; Jennifer Moyers, Production

    The Child's World®, Inc.: Mary Berendes, Publishing Director; Red Line Editorial, Fact Research; Cindy Klingel, Curriculum Advisor; Robert Noyed, Historical Advisor

Photos
    Cover: White House Collection, courtesy White House Historical Association; interior photographs are courtesy of the Lyndon Baines Johnson Library except as follows: Bettmann/Corbis: 12; John Fitzgerald Kennedy Library, Boston, MA: 25; ©Flip Schulke/Corbis 33; © Wally McNamee/Corbis: 37

Registration
    The Child's World®, Inc., Spirit of America™, and their associated logos are the sole property and registered trademarks of The Child's World®, Inc.

Library of Congress Cataloging-in-Publication Data
    Maupin, Melissa, 1958–
        Lyndon Baines Johnson : our thirty-sixth president / Melissa Maupin.
            p. cm.
        Includes bibliographical references and index.
        ISBN 1-56766-870-4 (lib. bdg. : alk. paper)
        1. Johnson, Lyndon B. (Lyndon Baines), 1908–1973—Juvenile literature. 2. Presidents—United States—Biography—Juvenile literature. [1. Johnson, Lyndon B. (Lyndon Baines), 1908–1973.
    2. Presidents.] I. Title.
        E847 .M38 2001
        973.923'092—dc21

                                                                00-011488

Contents

Chapter ONE

Farm Boy to Politician

Lyndon Baines Johnson was born in 1908 in the small town of Stonewall, Texas. His family had little money, and Lyndon had to work hard to achieve success.

LYNDON BAINES JOHNSON WAS THE FIRSTBORN child of Sam and Rebekah Johnson. He was born on a humble farm outside the town of Stonewall, Texas, on August 27, 1908. The family moved to Johnson City a few years later. Lyndon had three sisters, Rebekah, Lucia, Josefa, and a little brother named Sam.

Mr. Johnson was a farmer, but money was often in short supply. He spent more time dabbling in politics—the work of the government—than he did working on his farm. The family often struggled to make ends meet. Mrs. Johnson was well educated. She disliked being poor and wanted more for her children. She pushed Lyndon to study hard in school, hoping he would be successful one day.

Lyndon was a bright child but not a brilliant student. He excelled in English and history but barely scraped by in math and science. In high school, he was a prankster who stayed out late at night and sometimes cut classes. Lyndon always preferred the company of adults and older children. His friends were often 5 to 10 years older than he was.

Lyndon graduated from high school when he was 15. One night, he and his friends went out in his father's car and drank some beer. They ended up crashing the car, and Lyndon knew his dad would be furious. To escape punishment, Lyndon fled to a cousin's house near Corpus Christi, a town on the Texas coast. He got a job working in a cotton gin but found the work too difficult. He longed to return home.

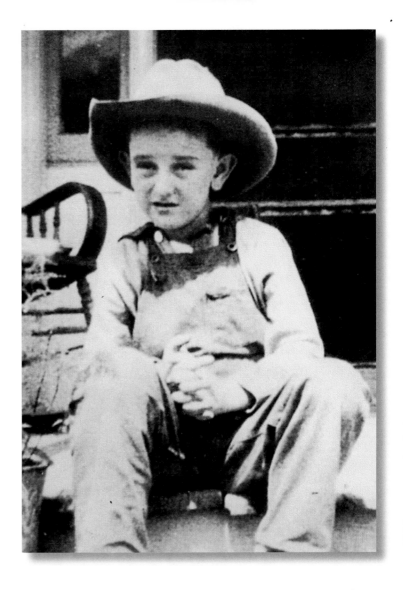

At age four, Lyndon would run to the local schoolhouse each day to play with his older cousins during recess. His mother soon convinced the teacher to let him take lessons, too. Lyndon had to help his parents at a young age. He worked as a shoeshine boy and trapped animals to earn money for the family.

Sam Ealy Johnson was a poor farmer, but he was also a lawmaker in the Texas government. Lyndon liked to listen to his father talk about politics. Rebekah Johnson was an educated woman. Before she married Lyndon's father, she worked as a reporter for a newspaper to pay her way through college.

After his father promised he would not punish him, Lyndon returned home. His mother urged him to settle down and attend Southwest Texas State Teachers College, the college closest to their home. But Lyndon was young and restless. He yearned to see the rest of the country.

Lyndon and several of his friends decided to take a road trip to California. Each boy pitched in five dollars to buy an old Model T car. They worked all along the trip doing odd jobs.

8

Once the boys arrived in California, Lyndon took several jobs, including working as an errand boy for a relative in a law firm.

When Lyndon returned to Texas, he got a job building a highway with a road gang. He earned two dollars a day. He finally signed up for college as his mother wished. As he attended classes, Lyndon also worked at the college to pay for his education. He started as a janitor but set his sights on better jobs. He used his early political skills to charm the staff. Soon he was the assistant to the secretary of the college president.

Lyndon left school for a year to teach students at Welhausen Ward Elementary School in Cotulla, Texas, near the Mexican border. His students were Mexicans and Mexican American children. They were even poorer than Lyndon had been as a child.

The school had little money to spend on its students. Unlike "white" schools, Welhausen offered only a very basic education. The students did not partici-pate in sports or other activities. Lyndon saw how unfair this was. He felt moved to improve the lives and education of his

Although Lyndon worked hard, he did find time for fun. He is shown here at bat.

9

students. He held **debates** and set up spelling bees in his classroom. He found money to buy sporting equipment. He hosted baseball games and track meets for the students.

At this early stage in his career, Lyndon Johnson decided that everyone had the right to a better life if they were willing to work for it. Later, as president, he told Americans about a plan to help the nation, which he called the "Great Society." He described the Great Society as "a place where the meaning of a man's life matches the marvels of a man's labor."

After working as a teacher for a year, Lyndon returned to college. He soon found he was more successful with the adults on campus than with the students. Most of the popular students at Southwest Texas College belonged to a group called the Black Stars. They had a lot of power on campus. Lyndon was considered odd looking, however. He was tall, skinny, and had big ears. Unlike many of the popular boys in the Black Stars, Lyndon was not an athlete. The Black Stars didn't want anything to do with him. But Lyndon fought back by forming the

White Stars. This group included many students who were outcasts on campus. The White Stars grew in number and power. Soon the White Stars were more powerful on campus than the Black Stars.

Lyndon was an average student in college. He enjoyed writing for the campus paper, *The Star*. As a member of the debate team, he was also a skilled speaker. Just before Lyndon's graduation, a young **politician** named Welly K. Hopkins heard him give a speech. Hopkins liked the speech so much that he asked Lyndon to help with his **campaign.** Lyndon eagerly made flyers and posters for Hopkins. He asked the White Stars to help him. Hopkins won the election and gave Lyndon much of the credit.

After graduation, Lyndon took a job teaching at Sam Houston High School. One day, he received a call from Richard Kleberg, a U.S. congressman from Texas. Kleberg had talked to Hopkins and heard what a great job Lyndon had done on his campaign. Kleberg asked Lyndon to be his secretary. Lyndon eagerly accepted, and at age 23, he made his first trip to Washington, D.C.

Interesting Facts

▸ Johnson City, where President Johnson lived as a boy, was named after James Johnson, the nephew of Lyndon's grandfather. James Johnson was the founder of the town.

▸ Lyndon Baines Johnson is often called simply "LBJ."

LYNDON JOHNSON WAS A COLORFUL MAN. HE STOOD SIX FEET THREE INCHES tall, had big ears, and often wore cowboy boots. His looks, his Texas drawl, and his strong personality made him hard to forget. But Johnson never left anything to chance. To make sure future generations remembered him, Johnson left his name on the LBJ School of Public Affairs, the LBJ Library and Museum, and the LBJ National Park.

The LBJ School of Public Affairs and the LBJ Library and Museum are located at the University of Texas in Austin. Johnson was proud of both organizations. The School of Public Affairs is for students who are planning a life in public service. Johnson wanted real-life politicians to teach the students instead of professors. The LBJ Library and Museum is one of the nation's many presidential libraries. It is eight stories high and houses 44 million documents from Johnson's career. Johnson said of the library, "I hope that visitors who come here will achieve a closer understanding of the presidency and that the young people who come here will get a clearer comprehension of what this nation tried to do in an eventful period of its history."

Shortly after Johnson retired, he and his wife donated a portion of the LBJ Ranch to the National Park Service. Johnson had turned his land into a successful working ranch with 400 head of cattle. He asked the park service to keep his ranch working. Today the ranch, the Johnson's home, the family cemetery, and the one-room schoolhouse where Johnson started school are part of one section of the Lyndon Baines Johnson National Park. Another section of the park is 14 miles away in Johnson City. It includes the Johnson settlement, his boyhood home, and a visitor center.

Chapter TWO

Life in Washington

Johnson worked for Congressman Kleberg for three years. During that time, he learned how Congress worked. He began to plan for a career in politics.

WHILE WORKING AS SECRETARY TO CONGRESS-man Kleberg, Johnson met Claudia Alta Taylor, a lovely young woman from Texas. Claudia was nicknamed "Lady Bird" because her nanny once said she was as pretty as a lady bird. She was from one of the wealthiest families in eastern Texas. A shy, intelligent woman, Lady Bird had graduated from the University of Texas where, like Lyndon, she had worked on the campus newspaper. Lyndon Johnson fell in love with her at first sight and proposed to her on their first date. Lady Bird later said she was totally surprised at his proposal. "I thought it was some kind of a joke," she recalled.

Lyndon Johnson returned to Washington, but the couple kept in touch with letters and phone calls. Just seven weeks later, on

November 17, 1934, Johnson turned his proposal into a life-long commitment. He came back to Texas and insisted that Lady Bird marry him that very day. Flustered but also in love, she agreed. The ceremony hastily took place at Saint Mark's Episcopal Church in San Antonio. After the honeymoon, Lady Bird moved with Johnson to Washington.

Johnson met Claudia Alta Taylor on a trip home to Texas. He decided almost instantly that she should be his wife. Less than two months later, Lady Bird, as her friends and family called her, agreed to marry him. They wed in Texas on November 17, 1934. This photograph was taken during their honeymoon in Mexico.

Not long after their wedding, Congressman Kleberg fired Johnson. Rumor had it that Kleberg feared Johnson was after his job. Johnson wasn't unemployed for long, however. Friends recommended him for the National Youth Administration (NYA). The NYA was one of the many programs that President Franklin Roosevelt had begun to help the unemployed Americans during the **Great Depression.**

The Johnsons moved back home to Texas, where Lyndon would act as director of the state's NYA program.

Johnson was successful at his new job. Word spread that he was a man of action. In 1937, Johnson heard there was an opening in the U.S. Congress. He decided the time was right to run for office. He ran as a member of the Democratic Party, one of the two most powerful **political parties** in the country.

The election for Congress was tough. Eight other **candidates** from his area were running. Johnson searched for a way to stand out from the crowd. He claimed that he was the only candidate who truly supported President Roosevelt and his work. Roosevelt was a very popular president. Johnson's idea won him a seat in the House of Representatives.

In 1940, Johnson ran for his seat in the House again. Although he won, he soon realized that it would be years before he had enough **seniority** to make important decisions. In April of the following year, he saw an opportunity to move ahead. Morris Sheppard, a U.S. senator from Texas, had died. His seat in the Senate was open.

Johnson decided to run for the position. This meant he had to campaign all across the big state of Texas.

To reach voters, Johnson used radio ads. He was doing well until the governor of Texas, W. Lee "Pappy" O'Daniel, entered the race. This upset Johnson, who knew that O'Daniel was popular and well known. Still, Johnson was ahead the night of the election, and he even celebrated his victory. But when the votes were counted the next day, he learned that O'Daniel had won. Johnson and his supporters thought O'Daniel's people might have cheated, but they could not prove it.

Johnson didn't have time to feel sorry for himself. World War II was exploding in Europe. On December 7, 1941, the Japanese bombed Pearl Harbor in Hawaii. The United States entered the war the next day. Johnson, still a member of the House, was the first congressman who volunteered to serve. As a lieutenant commander in the U.S. Navy, Johnson proved he was brave and strong. After a heroic air battle with the Japanese, General Douglas MacArthur

Interesting Facts

▶ After being reelected to the House of Representatives in 1940, Johnson celebrated his victory from a hospital bed. He was recovering from an appendicitis operation.

▶ Lady Bird ran Lyndon's congressional office while he was in the navy.

Johnson (second from right) became the first congressman to volunteer for active duty in the military. He reported for duty in the U.S. Navy on December 9, 1941— two days after the bombing of Pearl Harbor.

awarded Johnson the Silver Star, the third highest medal of valor in the armed forces.

One year later, President Roosevelt called all congressmen in the military back to the United States. It was time for them to return to work. Johnson's war experiences would help shape the ideas he held as president many years later, when the nation was struggling with the Vietnam War. "I learned that war comes about by two things," he said, "by a lust for power on the part of a few evil leaders and by a weakness on the part of the people whose love for peace too often displays a lack of courage that serves as an open invitation to all the aggressors of the world."

As Johnson returned to his work in Congress, he began to save money and make investments, such as buying property. The poverty of his youth had always haunted him. He wanted a secure life for him and for his family. Lynda Bird, the Johnson's first child, was born in 1944. Their second daughter, Luci Baines, arrived in 1947.

In 1948, Johnson won his first **term** in the Senate. As a young senator, he again was frustrated that he had so little power. The "inner club" made most of the decisions. It included powerful senators who had served for many years. Johnson thought he might gain power by seeking a position of leadership in the Democratic Party. He asked his friend Senator Richard Russell to help him. Russell praised Johnson's abilities when he talked with the inner club. In 1953, Johnson was voted the Senate minority leader. The minority leader takes charge of the political

Johnson held many important positions of leadership during his years in the Senate. He was a senator from 1949 to 1961.

party with the fewest members in the Senate. He was the youngest senator to ever hold such an important position.

In 1954, Johnson was reelected to the Senate. He was named the majority leader. (After the election of 1954, there were more Democrats than Republicans in the Senate.) At last Johnson had the power he desired, but his work was very stressful. In 1955, it took a toll on his health. He suffered a major heart attack and spent four months recovering. He rested at the LBJ Ranch, a piece of land outside of Austin, Texas, that he had bought in the late 1940s.

After his health improved, Johnson returned to work. He helped pass the **Civil Rights** Act of 1957. He also led a committee to advance space exploration. The committee pushed through the Space Act of 1958, which created the National Aeronautics and Space Administration (NASA).

LYNDON JOHNSON WAS known for his powerful style of leadership. Many people called him an "operator" because he knew how to get things done—and done his way. Johnson had learned to get what he wanted by talking to the right people and saying the right things.

As president, Johnson wanted to pass his bills in Congress. He found out which members of Congress were against certain bills and why. Johnson then met with them and used his political skills to talk them into voting for his programs.

Although he was successful at working with Congress, Johnson sometimes ignored his staff and other people who helped him. The newspapers often talked about President Johnson's powerful style of leadership. They compared him to a king who ordered others to do as he commanded. Johnson didn't mind this talk. Such remarks did upset those who worked with the president, however. They wanted credit for helping him pass his programs through Congress and for helping him succeed.

Chapter THREE

Into the White House

When Johnson became vice president in 1961, he had no idea that tragic events would force him to take over the presidency.

IN 1960, LYNDON JOHNSON WAS A RECOGNIZED leader of his party. He decided to make a run for the presidency. Although his campaign slogan became, "All the way with LBJ," Johnson was actually unsure whether he was ready to lead the nation. At the 1960 Democratic National Convention, members of the party had to choose their presidential candidate. They seemed to agree that Johnson wasn't ready and selected John F. Kennedy instead.

The party members then began to talk about choosing Johnson as the vice presidential candidate. Lady Bird Johnson approved of this idea. She was concerned about her husband's health. She believed that the job of vice president would be less stressful than her husband's position in the Senate. When John Kennedy

asked Johnson to run with him, he gladly accepted. Kennedy and Johnson proved to be winners with American voters. In January of 1961, Johnson was sworn in as vice president of the United States.

Johnson played an active role as vice president. Like most leaders in this position, he traveled to spread the word about the president's plans and programs. But Johnson traveled more than most. He visited 34 countries.

Johnson and Kennedy traveled around the country, campaigning to win the election of 1960.

He also served as chairman on two important committees, the President's Committee on Equal Employment Opportunity and the National Aeronautics and Space Council.

By 1963, the popular Kennedy-Johnson team began campaigning for the election of 1964. Unfortunately, on November 22, they made a fateful stop in Dallas, Texas. The president and first lady were riding in an open convertible car. Johnson was riding just two cars behind the president when tragedy struck. A man named Lee Harvey Oswald shot and killed President Kennedy. Like all U.S. citizens, Johnson was stunned and deeply saddened by Kennedy's **assassination.**

Just hours after Kennedy's death, Johnson took the oath of office as president of the United States. Five days later, he

Kennedy and Johnson were a strong pair, and they planned to run again in the election of 1964.

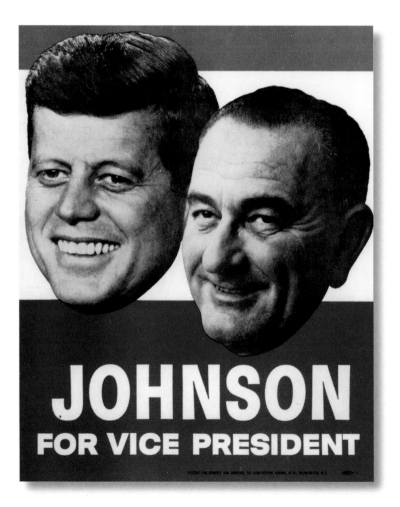

24

addressed the nation on television. He vowed to carry out all of Kennedy's programs. One important goal was civil rights for all Americans. Kennedy wanted to end **discrimination** against blacks and other minorities in the country. President Johnson pleaded with the country to put their differences aside in memory of the late President Kennedy. "Let us put an end to the teaching and preaching of hate and evil and violence," he said.

Interesting Facts

▸ After President Kennedy's assassination, Lyndon B. Johnson took the oath of office aboard the presidential airplane, *Air Force One.* Mrs. Johnson and Jacqueline Kennedy stood beside him.

On November 22, 1963, Lyndon Baines Johnson became the 36th president of the United States following the assassination of John F. Kennedy. When Johnson addressed Congress five days later, he said, "All I have I would have gladly given not to be standing here today. The greatest leader of our time has been struck down by the foulest deed of our time.… An assassin's bullet has thrust upon me the awesome burden of the presidency."

The first issue President Johnson tackled was a **tax** cut, which would lower the taxes Americans had to pay. Some senators argued that this didn't make sense because the government needed all the money it earned from taxes. Johnson looked at the nation's **budget** and cut wasteful spending from every department. In fact, he cut $500 million dollars from the budget! Congress finally agreed there was enough money for his tax cut.

Next, Johnson pushed through the Civil Rights Act of 1964. This ended **segregation** laws that discriminated against African Americans. Segregation laws kept blacks from entering certain public places that were reserved for whites only, such as restrooms, hotels, and restaurants. The Civil Rights Act made such laws illegal. But even with this act, problems with discrimination continued. African Americans still struggled for equal rights.

Another difficult issue that President Johnson faced was the war in Vietnam. U.S. involvement in the war had begun long before Johnson became president. During President Harry Truman's term, the

Johnson signed the Civil Rights Act of 1964 on June 2. This act ended segregation laws in the United States.

United States had given money to France, which was the ruler of Vietnam at the time. Rebels led by a man named Ho Chi Minh began to fight against the French. They wanted to turn Vietnam into a **communist** country. During the rebellion, Vietnam divided into two countries: North Vietnam, which was communist, and South Vietnam, which was striving to build a **democracy,** like the United States.

War continued between the countries. Both Presidents Eisenhower and Kennedy

The most difficult challenge of Johnson's presidency was the war in Vietnam, which raged throughout his six years in office. He is shown here (standing at left in the vehicle) with General William Westmoreland (standing to the right of Johnson) during a 1966 tour of Vietnam.

had sent money to help South Vietnam. President Kennedy also had sent 17,000 military advisers. They hoped to stop the spread of communism around the world. Johnson continued sending money, but he did not send any troops—at first.

During the 1964 presidential campaign, the North Vietnamese bombed an American destroyer in the Gulf of Tonkin. Johnson then ordered the bombing of Vietnamese boats and bases. He asked Congress to pass the Gulf of Tonkin Resolution. This act would allow him to take military action in Vietnam without actually declaring war. Looking back, many people believe that this action moved the United States toward a full war in Vietnam.

President Johnson felt confident as he continued his campaign for his first elected term as president. He told the people that the United States had "the opportunity to move not only toward the rich society and powerful society, but upward to the Great Society." He saw a strong, successful country for all people. "The Great Society rests on abundance and liberty for all," he told voters. "It demands an end to poverty and racial injustice."

The Republican Party chose Barry Goldwater as its candidate. Goldwater talked of using nuclear weapons on communist countries such as the Soviet Union and Vietnam. These powerful weapons could cause terrible destruction all over the world. Goldwater frightened many Americans. Their support for Johnson showed as they cast their votes that year.

Just before the election, President and Mrs. Johnson went to Texas to await the results. "It seems to me tonight that I have spent my whole life getting ready for this moment," Johnson said. When the votes were counted, he had won the election by a landslide. His supporters were rich and poor, from all walks of life and every race.

29

Chapter FOUR

A Trying End

President Johnson hoped to do great things for Americans, improving the lives of the poor and pushing for equal rights. Although he had great hope for the future, his presidency was filled with difficult challenges.

LYNDON JOHNSON BEGAN HIS FIRST ELECTED term as president dedicated to his idea of the Great Society. The first bill he signed was for a program called Medicare. The number of elderly people had doubled in the previous 20 years. Medicare gave people over the age of 65 health care that they could afford.

Johnson followed this new law with one to increase funds for schools. He remembered his own experiences teaching poor children in Texas. He realized that education had helped him get all the way to the White House. President Kennedy had tried to pass a similar bill for a year without success. Johnson used his political skills to get it passed in just 87 days.

Despite his efforts to ensure civil rights for blacks, racial problems continued to

30

grow worse. In the South, whites threatened blacks when they tried to enter courthouses to vote. Law enforcement officers often stopped blacks from voting as well. A civil rights leader named Martin Luther King Jr. began to organize his people to **protest** these actions. He encouraged African Americans to register to vote. In 1965, in Selma, Alabama, King led a drive to register three million black voters. The sheriff, Jim Clark, arrested many of them. Police officers clubbed or beat others.

King did not back down. He organized a march of black and white people from Selma to the state capital of Montgomery in protest.

On July 30, 1965, Johnson signed the Medicare bill in a ceremony at the Harry S. Truman Library in Independence, Missouri. The act established a government-run medical care program for the elderly. Former President Truman is seated at right.

31

▸ Near the end of his presidency, Johnson's popularity dropped. News stories began to criticize his policies. Johnson followed the news carefully to learn the public's opinion of him.

▸ As first lady, Mrs. Johnson was an environmentalist. She planted beautiful flower gardens at the White House and talked others into planting gardens around Washington. In 1965, she helped start the Highway Beautification Act, which removed billboards and junkyards from the countryside.

Sheriff Clark ordered the protesters to stop, but they did not. Clark and his men rode into the crowd and severely beat the people. They fired tear gas to break up the group.

King planned another march for two weeks later. President Johnson was unsure what to do. He wanted to protect the marchers with government troops, yet he didn't want to send in troops against the wishes of Alabama Governor George Wallace. Doing so would only make Wallace a hero to other whites who were **prejudiced** against blacks. Johnson met with Wallace. He convinced Wallace that protecting the marchers was in his best interest. Wallace finally agreed to ask for federal troops, and the march proceeded peacefully.

The civil rights struggle inspired Johnson to create the most important act of his time in office: the Voting Rights Act. This allowed the national government to supervise elections, making sure that all Americans would be able to vote. Johnson asked Congress to pass the bill by saying that the freedom promised in the U.S. **Constitution** was for every American citizen. Congress passed the bill in 1965.

Although Johnson had success with his
Great Society program, he had serious trouble
with the Vietnam War. By the mid-1960s, it
looked as if South Vietnam would lose the war.
In February of 1965, the enemy attacked a U.S.
airstrip in South Vietnam, killing eight Americans.
President Johnson ordered a bombing. But unlike
earlier ones, he did not stop. He continued the
bombing for weeks. A month later, Johnson
began to send ground troops to Vietnam.

Although Johnson made the struggle for civil rights an important part of his presidency, racial problems continued. People gathered in cities all over the South to protest discrimination.

Soon thousands of young men were sent to help the South Vietnamese fight against the communists. Congress still never formally declared that the United States was at war.

Sending U.S. troops to Vietnam did not work. It only resulted in more deaths on both sides. But Johnson felt he had to continue. He worried that if he didn't, the war might turn into World War III. Although most Americans agreed with him at first, many grew tired of the senseless waste of human life. People began to protest U.S. involvement in the war as President Johnson devoted more time to winning it.

As the 1968 election grew near, Johnson studied his chances for reelection. Senator Eugene McCarthy had entered as a Democrat with an antiwar message. President Kennedy's brother, Senator Robert Kennedy, also joined the contest. Johnson felt he still might win, but he needed to concentrate on the war, not on the election. His past health problems also worried him.

On March 31, Johnson addressed the nation on television. He said, "I shall not seek, and will not accept, the **nomination** of my

34

party for another term as your president." He added that he would greatly reduce the bombing of North Vietnam in an effort to end the war.

Several days after Johnson's announcement, North Vietnam leaders said they were willing to begin peace talks. The news relieved Johnson, but bad news quickly followed. Martin Luther King Jr. was assassinated in Memphis. As the shocked public reacted, Johnson used the sad event to further advance the civil rights cause. He passed a bill that had been stalled for two years—The Civil Rights Act of 1968. This act stopped homeowners from discriminating against buyers because of their race. The bill passed just three days after Martin Luther King's funeral.

On October 31, the United States and North Vietnam began peace talks in Paris. But the war would continue for five more years.

Lyndon Johnson dropped out of public life after Republican Richard Nixon became president in 1969. He spent his retirement with Lady Bird, his daughters, and his grandchildren. He worked on writing his memoirs (the story of his life) and founded the LBJ Library and Museum in Austin.

Even after a difficult term, Johnson had faith in the presidency. "No president in history has been able to do all the things that he or the people hoped he could accomplish at the time of election," Johnson once said. "But that doesn't mean that the job is impossible."

Johnson suffered chest pains in 1970 and a second heart attack in 1972. He recuperated again at the LBJ Ranch in Texas. Early the next year, President Nixon announced a cease-fire with North Vietnam. As the United States prepared to withdraw from the war, Lyndon Baines Johnson died on January 22, 1973 from a fatal heart attack. He was buried on the LBJ Ranch in next to the graves of his mother and father.

THE VIETNAM WAR WAS THE MOST DIFFICULT ISSUE OF PRESIDENT JOHNSON'S presidency. Even though he had great success with civil rights, many people only recall his problems with the war. By 1966, Johnson had sent nearly 400,000 American soldiers into battle and was bombing North Vietnam. Suddenly, his Great Society programs came second to winning the war.

By 1967, President Johnson believed that the United States was close to a victory. He also believed that the American people would stand behind him. Many Americans grew angry that the war was dragging on. Antiwar protests broke out in cities across the country. People did not want to see Americans die for a war that had little to do with the United States. Protesters often chanted, "Hey, hey, LBJ! How many kids did you kill today?"

By 1967, more than half of Americans were against President Johnson's Vietnam policies. Still, Johnson told the public that the war was going well. He told them that the North Vietnamese were a small force that would soon lose. But on January 31, 1968, the North Vietnamese surprised the United States with a huge attack called the Tet Offensive. It took place during the Tet holidays that celebrated the Vietnamese New Year. The North Vietnamese attacked 31 South Vietnamese cities and the American embassy.

Two thousand Americans died in the Tet Offensive. U.S. citizens realized that the North Vietnamese were not weak and small. They felt President Johnson had misled them. His popularity dropped. Johnson announced that he would not seek a second term in 1968. He felt he needed to concentrate on winning the war instead of a campaign. The Vietnam War finally ended in 1973, the same year that Lyndon Johnson died.

1908 Lyndon Johnson is born on August 27 on a farm outside of Stonewall, Texas.

1913 The Johnson family moves to nearby Johnson City.

1924 At age 15, Lyndon graduates from Johnson City High School.

1927 Lyndon enrolls in Southwest Texas State Teachers College in San Marcos, Texas.

1930 On August 19, Johnson graduates from college with a degree in education.

1931 Congressman Richard Kleberg asks Johnson to come to Washington to work as his secretary.

1934 Johnson meets and falls in love with Claudia Alta (Lady Bird) Taylor. On November 17, they marry in San Antonio, Texas.

1935 Johnson is named the Texas director of President Roosevelt's National Youth Administration.

1937 Johnson is elected to the U.S. House of Representatives.

1940 Johnson is reelected to the House of Representatives.

1941 Johnson loses the election for the U.S. Senate. The Japanese bomb Pearl Harbor on December 7. Johnson, still a member of the House of Representatives, becomes the first member of Congress to volunteer for active duty in the armed forces.

1942 Johnson receives the Silver Star from General Douglas MacArthur for bravery in action during an air combat mission. President Franklin Roosevelt orders all members of Congress in the armed forces to return to their offices.

1948 In November, Johnson wins election to the U.S. Senate.

1953 On January 2, Johnson is voted minority leader of the Senate. He is the youngest man to ever hold this position.

1954 On November 2, Johnson is reelected to the Senate for a second term.

1955 Johnson is elected majority leader of the Senate. He is the youngest man to ever hold this position. He suffers his first heart attack and spends four months recovering.

1957 Johnson helps the Senate pass the Civil Rights Act of 1957.

1958 Johnson leads the Senate committee that helps establish the National Aeronautics and Space Administration (NASA).

1960 Johnson is elected vice president of the United States on November 8. He is reelected to the Senate at the same time.

1961 Johnson is named President Kennedy's chairman of the National Aeronautics and Space Council.

1963 On November 22 President Kennedy is assassinated in Dallas, Texas. Lyndon Baines Johnson becomes the 36th president of the United States.

1964 Johnson signs the Civil Rights Act of 1964. Congress passes the Gulf of Tonkin Resolution. Johnson is nominated for president of the United States at the Democratic National Convention. On November 3, he is elected president of the United States. Hubert Humphrey is elected vice president.

1965 President Johnson takes the oath of office on January 20. He begins sending additional troops to Vietnam in the spring. On July 30, he signs the Medicare bill. On August 6, he signs the Voting Rights Act, which he later cites as the most important accomplishment of his presidency.

1968 Johnson announces that he will not be a candidate for another term as president of the United States, in part because he wants to devote his time to ending the war, not to the election. Martin Luther King Jr. is assassinated in April. The Civil Rights Act is passed. The U.S. and North Vietnam begin peace talks in October.

1969 On January 20, Johnson returns to Texas and the LBJ Ranch after Richard M. Nixon is sworn in as president.

1971 On May 22, Johnson attends the dedication of the Lyndon Baines Johnson Library and Museum on the campus of the University of Texas at Austin.

1973 Lyndon Johnson dies at his ranch on January 22. He is buried in the family cemetery at the LBJ Ranch near his birthplace. U.S. participation in the Vietnam War ends.

assassination (uh-sass-ih-NAY-shun)
An assassination is the murder of a someone, especially a well-known person. Johnson became president after the assassination of President John Kennedy.

budget (BUJ-it)
A budget is a plan to make the best use of money. Johnson looked at the nation's budget and cut wasteful spending from every department.

campaign (kam-PAYN)
A campaign is the process of running for an election, including activities such as giving speeches or attending rallies. Welly K. Hopkins asked Johnson to help with his campaign.

candidates (KAN-dih-detz)
Candidates are people running in an election. Nine candidates were running for the open seat in Congress in 1937.

civil rights (SIH-vel RYTZ)
Civil rights are the rights guaranteed by the Constitution to all citizens of the United States. Johnson helped pass the Civil Rights Act of 1957.

communist (KOM-yeh-nist)
In a communist country, the government, not the people, holds all the power, and there is no private ownership of property. North Vietnam was a communist country.

constitution (kon-stih-TOO-shun)
A constitution is the set of basic principles that govern a state, country, or society. The U.S. Constitution promises certain rights to American citizens.

debates (deh-BAYTZ)
Debates are competitions in which people discuss a question or topic, considering reasons for and against it. Johnson held debates for his students when he was a teacher.

democracy (deh-MOK-reh-see)
A democracy is a country in which the people control the government by electing their own leaders. The United States is a democracy.

discrimination (dis-krim-ih-NAY-shun)
Discrimination is the unfair treatment of people simply because they are different. Johnson tried to carry on President Kennedy's goal of ending discrimination.

**Great Depression
(GREAT dee-PRESH-un)**
The Great Depression was a period in U.S. history when there was little business activity, and many people could not find work. President Franklin Roosevelt started the NYA to help the unemployed during the Great Depression.

nomination (nom-ih-NAY-shun)
If someone receives a nomination, he or she is chosen by a political party to run for office. Johnson did not seek the Democratic presidential nomination in 1968.

**political parties
(puh-LIT-ih-kul PAR-teez)**
Political parties are groups of people who share similar ideas about how to run a government. Johnson was a member of the Democratic political party.

politician (pawl-ih-TISH-un)
A politician is a person who holds an office in government. Lyndon Johnson was a politician.

prejudiced (PREJ-eh-dist)
If people are prejudiced, they have a bad opinion about someone without good reason. Johnson did not want to make Governor Wallace a hero to whites who were prejudiced against blacks.

protest (PROH-test)
If people protest something, they speak out to say that it is wrong. Martin Luther King Jr. organized people to protest discrimination against African Americans.

segregation (seh-grih-GAY-shun)
Segregation was the practice of using laws to keep black and white people apart. The Civil Rights Act of 1964 stopped segregation laws.

seniority (seen-YOR-ih-tee)
If people have seniority, they have held a position longer than other people. In Congress, members with seniority have the most power.

tax (TAX)
Tax is money paid by citizens to support their government. Johnson was in favor of a tax cut in 1964, which lowered taxes for Americans.

term (TERM)
A term is the length of time a politician can keep his or her position by law. A U.S. president's term is four years.

41

Our PRESIDENTS

President	Birthplace	Life Span	Presidency	Political Party	First Lady
George Washington	Virginia	1732–1799	1789–1797	None	Martha Dandridge Custis Washington
John Adams	Massachusetts	1735–1826	1797–1801	Federalist	Abigail Smith Adams
Thomas Jefferson	Virginia	1743–1826	1801–1809	Democratic-Republican	widower
James Madison	Virginia	1751–1836	1809–1817	Democratic Republican	Dolley Payne Todd Madison
James Monroe	Virginia	1758–1831	1817–1825	Democratic Republican	Elizabeth Kortright Monroe
John Quincy Adams	Massachusetts	1767–1848	1825–1829	Democratic-Republican	Louisa Johnson Adams
Andrew Jackson	South Carolina	1767–1845	1829–1837	Democrat	widower
Martin Van Buren	New York	1782–1862	1837–1841	Democrat	widower
William H. Harrison	Virginia	1773–1841	1841	Whig	Anna Symmes Harrison
John Tyler	Virginia	1790–1862	1841–1845	Whig	Letitia Christian Tyler / Julia Gardiner Tyler
James K. Polk	North Carolina	1795–1849	1845–1849	Democrat	Sarah Childress Polk

42

Our PRESIDENTS

President	Birthplace	Life Span	Presidency	Political Party	First Lady
Zachary Taylor	Virginia	1784–1850	1849–1850	Whig	Margaret Mackall Smith Taylor
Millard Fillmore	New York	1800–1874	1850–1853	Whig	Abigail Powers Fillmore
Franklin Pierce	New Hampshire	1804–1869	1853–1857	Democrat	Jane Means Appleton Pierce
James Buchanan	Pennsylvania	1791–1868	1857–1861	Democrat	never married
Abraham Lincoln	Kentucky	1809–1865	1861–1865	Republican	Mary Todd Lincoln
Andrew Johnson	North Carolina	1808–1875	1865–1869	Democrat	Eliza McCardle Johnson
Ulysses S. Grant	Ohio	1822–1885	1869–1877	Republican	Julia Dent Grant
Rutherford B. Hayes	Ohio	1822–1893	1877–1881	Republican	Lucy Webb Hayes
James A. Garfield	Ohio	1831–1881	1881	Republican	Lucretia Rudolph Garfield
Chester A. Arthur	Vermont	1829–1886	1881–1885	Republican	widower
Grover Cleveland	New Jersey	1837–1908	1885–1889	Democrat	Frances Folsom Cleveland

	President	Birthplace	Life Span	Presidency	Political Party	First Lady
	Benjamin Harrison	Ohio	1833–1901	1889–1893	Republican	Caroline Scott Harrison
	Grover Cleveland	New Jersey	1837–1908	1893–1897	Democrat	Frances Folsom Cleveland
	William McKinley	Ohio	1843–1901	1897–1901	Republican	Ida Saxton McKinley
	Theodore Roosevelt	New York	1858–1919	1901–1909	Republican	Edith Kermit Carow Roosevelt
	William H. Taft	Ohio	1857–1930	1909–1913	Republican	Helen Herron Taft
	Woodrow Wilson	Virginia	1856–1924	1913–1921	Democrat	Ellen L. Axson Wilson Edith Bolling Galt Wilson
	Warren G. Harding	Ohio	1865–1923	1921–1923	Republican	Florence Kling De Wolfe Harding
	Calvin Coolidge	Vermont	1872–1933	1923–1929	Republican	Grace Goodhue Coolidge
	Herbert C. Hoover	Iowa	1874–1964	1929–1933	Republican	Lou Henry Hoover
	Franklin D. Roosevelt	New York	1882–1945	1933–1945	Democrat	Anna Eleanor Roosevelt Roosevelt
	Harry S. Truman	Missouri	1884–1972	1945–1953	Democrat	Elizabeth Wallace Truman

President	Birthplace	Life Span	Presidency	Political Party	First Lady
Dwight D. Eisenhower	Texas	1890–1969	1953–1961	Republican	Mary "Mamie" Doud Eisenhower
John F. Kennedy	Massachusetts	1917–1963	1961–1963	Democrat	Jacqueline Bouvier Kennedy
Lyndon B. Johnson	Texas	1908–1973	1963–1969	Democrat	Claudia Alta Taylor Johnson
Richard M. Nixon	California	1913–1994	1969–1974	Republican	Thelma Catherine Ryan Nixon
Gerald Ford	Nebraska	1913–	1974–1977	Republican	Elizabeth "Betty" Bloomer Warren Ford
James Carter	Georgia	1924–	1977–1981	Democrat	Rosalynn Smith Carter
Ronald Reagan	Illinois	1911–	1981–1989	Republican	Nancy Davis Reagan
George Bush	Massachusetts	1924–	1989–1993	Republican	Barbara Pierce Bush
William Clinton	Arkansas	1946–	1993–2001	Democrat	Hillary Rodham Clinton
George W. Bush	Connecticut	1946–	2001–	Republican	Laura Welch Bush

Presidential FACTS

Qualifications

To run for president, a candidate must
- be at least 35 years old
- be a citizen who was born in the United States
- have lived in the United States for 14 years

Term of Office

A president's term of office is four years. No president can stay in office for more than two terms.

Election Date

The presidential election takes place every four years on the first Tuesday of November.

Inauguration Date

Presidents are inaugurated on January 20.

Oath of Office

I do solemnly swear I will faithfully execute the office of the President of the United States and will to the best of my ability preserve, protect, and defend the Constitution of the United States.

Write a Letter to the President

One of the best things about being a U.S. citizen is that Americans get to participate in their government. They can speak out if they feel government leaders aren't doing their jobs. They can also praise leaders who are going the extra mile. Do you have something you'd like the president to do? Should the president worry more about the environment and encourage people to recycle? Should the government spend more money on our schools? You can write a letter to the president to say how you feel!

1600 Pennsylvania Avenue
Washington, D.C. 20500

You can even send an e-mail to: president@whitehouse.gov

46

For Further INFORMATION

Internet Sites

Learn more about Lyndon Johnson as president:
http://www.whitehouse.gov/WH/glimpse/presidents/html/lj36.html

Take a virtual stroll through the LBJ Library and Museum:
http://www.lbjlib.utexas.edu/

Read famous speeches given by President Johnson:
http://www.tamu.edu/scom/pres/speeches/lbj.html

Visit Johnson City, the area where LBJ was born and raised:
http://home1.gte.net/impekabl/jcpage.htm

Tour the LBJ National Park and learn more about Johnson's early life:
http://www.nps.gov/lyjo/home.htm

Learn more about Lady Bird Johnson:
http://www.lbjlib.utexas.edu/johnson/archives.hom/biographys.hom/ladybird_bio.asp

Learn more about all the presidents and visit the White House:
http://www.whitehouse.gov/WH/glimpse/presidents/html/presidents.html
http://www.thepresidency.org/presinfo.htm
http://www.americanpresidents.org/

Books

Eskow, Dennis. *Lyndon Baines Johnson.* New York: Franklin Watts, 1993.

Flynn, Jean. *The Story of Claudia Alta (Lady Bird) Johnson.* El Cajon, CA. Sunbelt Media, 1992.

Foster, Leila Merrell. *The Story of the Great Society.* Chicago: Childrens Press, 1991.

Harper, Judith E. *John F. Kennedy: Our Thirty-Fifth President.* Chanhassen, MN: The Child's World, 2002.

Healey, Tim. *The 1960s.* New York: Franklin Watts, 1988.

Kaye, Tony. *Johnson.* Philadelphia: Chelsea House Publishers, 1988.

Index